Mastering Habit - How Successful People Think And Operate

Adidas Wilson

Published by Adidas Wilson, 2019.

Copyright © 2019 by Adidas Wilson

All rights reserved. No part of this publication may be reproduced, distributed, or transmitted in any form or by any means, including photocopying, recording, or other electronic or mechanical methods, without the prior written permission of the publisher, except in the case of brief quotations embodied in critical reviews and certain other noncommercial uses permitted by copyright law. For permission requests, write to the publisher, addressed "Attention: Permissions Coordinator," at the address below.

Adidas Wilson
P.O. Box 2262
Antioch, Tn. 37011
siriusvisionstudios@gmail.com
www.financierpro.com

While every precaution has been taken in the preparation of this book, the publisher assumes no responsibility for errors or omissions, or for damages resulting from the use of the information contained herein.

MASTERING HABIT - HOW SUCCESSFUL PEOPLE THINK AND OPERATE

First edition. May 15, 2019.

Copyright © 2019 Adidas Wilson.

ISBN: 978-1386602958

Written by Adidas Wilson.

Disclaimer

THE AUTHOR HAS MADE every effort to ensure the accuracy of the information within this book was correct at time of publication. The author does not assume and hereby disclaims any liability to any party for any loss, damage, or disruption caused by errors or omissions, whether such errors or omissions result from accident, negligence, or any other cause.

Table of Contents

Introduction
    Ch. 1 - The Way of Happiness
    Ch. 2 - Steps for Building a Habit Stacking Routine
    Ch. 3 – What Makes Great Leadership
    Ch. 4 - 101 of the Greatest Insights and Actions for Work and Life
    Ch. 5 - The Secret to Living a Fulfilling Life
    Ch. 6 - Goals in Life
    Ch. 7 - Learning from Failure
    Ch. 8 – Create the Future You Visualize
    Ch. 9 - Innovation Personalities: Which One Are You?
    Ch. 10 – Self - Doubt
    Ch. 11 - Ambition VS. Talent
    Ch. 12 - Take 100% Responsibility for Your Life
    Ch. 13 - Self-Care
    Ch. 14 - Turn Stress into Success
    Ch. 15 – How Successful People Think and Operate
    Ch. 16 - Habits of Rich People
Conclusion

Introduction

Successful leaders know that any form of success is a process and not an event. They understand that success is cultivated; it is a daily commitment, a grind that is centered around the purpose of your life. To become an outstanding leader, there are habits that you must cultivate to build your reputation and success. As the habits become a part of you, you move closer to becoming a powerful leader. Daily reading comes with undeniable benefits. It offers free entertainment, enhances writing skills, improves concentration and focus, activates reasoning skills, improves memory, grows vocabulary, makes you more knowledgeable, reduces stress, enhances mental clarity, and makes you smarter. Reading is both stimulating and relaxing. Exceptional leaders thrive in the face of challenge. If you challenge yourself, you become more confident in doing it again. In addition to growing your knowledge and skills, confidence grows belief in yourself. Any competent leader knows the difference between a challenge that allows them to grow and one that will end in disaster. There are four levels of self-care; spiritual, mental, emotional, and physical. A great leader understands that their overall health affects every other area of their lives. To become a highly successful leader, take daily supplements, get enough sleep, eat well, and exercise regularly. In most cases, seasoned leaders are overachievers and can be too critical of themselves. To avoid being too harsh on yourself, find a mentor or someone you admire so you can consult them when the need arises. Planning your day, the night before is a very important successful habit. If you have no idea what you want to achieve, how can you become successful? Planning your day in advance helps you focus on details and tasks that make a difference in the bigger picture. Your day will begin in a smooth flow and you will be able to accomplish more. Most leaders emphasize on the importance of writing down your goals as you begin and revise them daily. Some encourage the reading of goals out aloud at least once a day. With your goals in front of you, your chances of succeeding increase. Keep refreshing the goals mentally so you can know whether you are still on the right path; otherwise, you may lose sight of your goal. In your comfort zone, things are comfortable and safer. Brilliant leaders, however, understand that they need to face the new and unfamiliar for them to grow and change. Regardless of the number of unknowns, take a risk from time to time; you do not have to win. Have an Inspiring and Powerful "Why" With a life purpose, you will live your life wholeheartedly and consciously. When you have a well-outlined "Why", everything you do (including the risks you take) becomes worth the effort.

"Whatever the mind of man can conceive and believe, it can achieve."

-Napoleon Hill

Chapter 1
The Way of Happiness

There are key happiness tactics and strategies that have shown to increase happiness. To be happy requires skills.

Happiness Is Not Supposed to Be Elusive

Happiness is not supposed to be an abstract ideal. Instead, it should be readily available wherever you go.

7 Principles of Happiness

- Focus on fulfillment
- Dedicate more time to your values
- Set a personal happiness level
- Drive from happiness
- Avoid the "if-then" trap
- Increase frustration tolerance
- Concentrate on purpose

Core Concepts

There are three primary concepts that are important in your happiness journey:

- Happiness is personal.

- Happiness is not static; it is a verb.

- There are two happiness questions: "How happy are you with your life?" and "how happy are you?"

Bonus Tactics

Strategies are effective but you need practical tactics for things to work out:

- Keep your eyes on the greater good.
- Act "as if".
- Cultivate happiness under you.
- Find your best happiness quotes.
- Look for a better metaphor (e.g. life is a dance).
- Adjust your questions for different results.
- Adjust your thoughts.

Take a closer look at the principles.

Focus on Fulfillment

When you focus on living life meaningfully, you will be more careful while making choices and creating moments. To do this, you must decide who you want to be and the kind of experiences you would like to create. If you want to focus on fulfilment, set your eyes on the greater good.

Dedicate More Time to Your Values

Living out your values helps you add happiness into your daily life. For people that spend the better part of their day working, try linking your job to your values. If excellence is important to you, make the work all about excellence. When more time is dedicated to your values, the journey becomes more enjoyable.

Set a Personal Happiness Level

Everyone has a personal happiness level. Embrace your level and begin from there. Look for simple ways through which you can improve your happiness level gradually. Avoid comparing your happiness levels to that of others.

Drive from Happiness

Happiness must be a decision.

Here, you must look deep within you and answer some very tough questions. What would you like to make more time for? What is it that makes you happy? What do you want to do? Instead of doing what everyone else expects of you, look for what makes you happy.

Avoid the "If-Then" Trap

Your happiness should not depend on an event that you expect to happen in the future, such as a relationship, job, etc. have your happiness "right here" rather than "out there". Have fun with the journey. Work with what you have.

Increase Your Frustration Tolerance

A higher frustration tolerance can translate to a higher happiness level. This insight works instantly. You just need to decide not to be frustrated with the little disappointments of life.

Concentrate on Purpose

What you focus on is what you get. Start focusing on better scenes and see what happens. Human beings set goals and do everything within their power to chase after them. They either attain the goals or drop dead. Once one goal has been achieved, they set another one and it goes on and on. This is how people are wired. America is in a time of abundance—much more like never in human history. Basic needs are generally met for everyone and, therefore, you think the only goals left to set are money goals. You aspire to earn a certain amount of income, build investments, and savings to a certain level and create a passive income stream. You set these goals so you can live the lifestyle of your choice and spend some time with your loved ones. You also want to be financially independent. To put it simply, you are trying to be happy and according to you, more money means happiness. Now, suppose you have all the money you desire in your bank account. You have finally achieved financial independence. You have enough time to spend with the ones you love, and you can go wherever you want—money is unlimited. Will you be happy? Sure, initially. However, once the ecstatic stage of travel, binge purchases and whatever else is over, you will be bored to death. You may find yourself lonely and depressed—something common to many famous and rich people. Why the unhappiness? Everyone wants to succeed, but success feels better when it is earned instead of undeservedly handed out. To be truly happy, you need to pursue and attain your lifestyle goals. This is common sense but how true is it? Some people pursue their goals, become successful but they are still unhappy. What is missing? You have a need to overcome your obstacles, accomplish, and achieve your goal. For human beings, the pursuit is the end, not the means to an end. Without it, you will be rich yet miserable, well-traveled yet depressed, financially independent yet bored. The lifestyle you seek reflects the connection you yearn for. For example, experiences are only full when shared with loved ones. To be happy, you need to integrate and balance your drive for pursuit and connection. Your love for the chase should be anchored to the reason for the chase. However, is that all there is to it? If you are successful in what you do and have healthy connections, will there be anything eating you up? Yes. There is one more piece to the puzzle. Once your basic needs (pursuit) and psychological needs (connection) have been fulfilled, the missing piece is self-actualization. To achieve total happiness, you must achieve your full potential and use your talents to the maximum. Calogero from a scene in *A Bronx Tale* says that: "the saddest thing in life is wasted talent, and the choices that you make will shape your life forever."

"THE MAJORITY OF MEN meet with failure of their lack of persistence in creating new plans to take the place of those which fail."
 -Napoleon Hill

Chapter 2
Steps for Building a Habit Stacking Routine

Will Durant said that you are what you repeatedly do. Habits have been proven to be efficient in creating positive change. The challenge is breaking the bad one and adding new habits. You can set yourself up for success by habit stacking or stacking habits. This involves taking small actions and linking them together to form a routine. Habit stacking allows you to make small changes which in turn lead to huge changes in your life. In habit stacking, performing the routine is key. The routine should consist of habits that flow simply. Repetition helps you build habits. The 8 steps below will help you create a habit stacking routine.

Choose a Time and Location

A routine is built around a specific time of day, location, or both. Here are a few examples:

- At home in the morning
- While working out at the gym
- While traveling
- During your lunch break

One Routine at a Time

You will be more motivated if you take on one routine at a time. Build one for a month then you can make whatever additions or changes you want.

Start with "Small Wins"

Where can you reap benefits from small wins? These areas can be divided into seven categories:

- Leisure
- Health/physical fitness
- Spirituality/well-being
- Organization
- Finances
- Relationships
- Productivity

Come Up with a Logical Checklist

A small checklist of actions and habits will help you accomplish individual habits. The habits should flow seamlessly and work together.

A Reason "Why"

Behind every action, have a good reason to keep you from quitting. For some people, habit stacking techniques help create time for their families.

Be Accountable

Doing nothing is easier than doing anything. Experts recommend letting other people in on your progress for accountability.

Have Small, Enjoyable Rewards

Award yourself when you complete a month, week or even a day of routine. The rewards should be small and have a positive impact.

Focus on Repetition

When you repeat a routine, your muscle memory grows. Focus on repetition especially on the first 30 days.

Dealing with Habits Stacking Challenges and Disruptions

Expect slip ups, disruptions and setbacks. What will you do when they arise? How quickly can you get up and get back on track? Check out these awesome strategies that can help you tackle your disruptions and go back to habit stacking: Have an if-then plan you cannot avoid disruptions. When these triggers occur, you need to have a plan. Do not allow them to discourage you. Forgive yourself and get ready to go on. Know your triggers: for you to create the plan, you must know what triggers you. Triggers include your bad habits and distractions that cause you to slip up. Reduce your expectations: when you exert too much pressure on yourself, you can have a negative reaction. Focus, instead, on the minimum while still concentrating on the most important habits. Start small (again): it can be discouraging to start over. However, that is what success is all about.

"ALL OUR DREAMS CAN come true if we have the courage to pursue them."

- *Walt Disney*

Chapter 3
What Makes Great Leadership

Leading a team of young, vibrant, and enthusiastic individuals might prove to be a daunting task, so that it is often difficult to make successful leaders of everyone. And while not everyone is built to take up leadership positions, there is always that one, or more, member of your team you feel is set up for the inevitable eventually. Those members of your team who mirror certain potentials of everything you possess as a leader, and that it is only a matter of time before they become one. But leadership is like fine art; it takes a lot of time, persistence, learning and unlearning, to become successful at it. And here's the question, how do you make the best leaders out of such people and make them better versions of yourself, bearing in mind that there are certain inadequacies of yourself you do not want to transfer to them too? There are different arguments on whether leadership is an innate ability or a thing that can be nurtured. The answer to this is irrelevant when you are trying to make new leaders of your team. No one starts to succeed at leadership immediately. Think Walt Disney and Henry Ford. Good leadership requires a lot of qualities, many that requires you learn them. While there is no singular way to raise new leaders, the following tips should help you make the best of raising a competent leader in your team.

Pragmatist or Idealist: Creating A Balance

Many teams and organizations contain different kinds of people and from different backgrounds. Some of which makes us unique in how we make certain decisions. As a leader, you already know that members of your team are either pragmatic or idealist (which is good for your team as there's no one way to get work done). But which category do

MASTERING HABIT - HOW SUCCESSFUL PEOPLE THINK AND OPERATE

your potential leaders fall into? Have they shown tendencies to become pragmatic leaders who believe in making decisions on the practical, rather than theoretical aspects of goals or objectives? Or an idealist leader who is more likely to float with "what happens in the end is all that matters" and that all goals can be met. In this case, as a leader, who is also a mentor now, you should make serious efforts to creating the best of leaders. He or she must realize that life is not a one-way lane and that compromises must be met sometimes. It may be dangerous to be on the extreme in whatever school of thought they belong to. And this is what Pravin Gordhan, a South African Politician and its former minister of finance, echoes when he says about leadership and the world requiring special kind of leaders, "...who balance romantic idealism, which is important, with pragmatism that converts the idealism into reality." Results indeed matter to a leader, but special and great leaders must be able to create a balance in whatever frameworks they have laid down to reaching a set goal. The journey to be a great leader is a tiring one, as you, the leader, already knows. And occasional failures, sometimes many, are major ingredients of what makes it so weary. But it is what births many great success stories. It won't be surprising, however, to find some members of your team unreceptive to failure. You must therefore make your prodigy(s) realize that failure is an inevitability if they want to be successful leaders. A great leader is someone who has failed in one capacity or the other before. Robert F. Kennedy, before he died, once said, "Only those who to fail greatly can ever achieve greatly." Now, this is not to excuse failure, it is to help emerging leaders have a consciousness of the reality of failure and that they would encounter it more than once when they become leaders. It is true that no one wants to fail, but it is also true that we fail, so that we may succeed most times. In the same vein, you must help those by discussing whatever failures they have had. The why? How? What should be done? questions must be asked and discussed among members of the team. No one should feel inadequate for making mistakes or failing blatantly. It is okay to want to oversee everything that goes on in your team in a bid to see that things are properly done. But sometimes, when raising a new leader, you just need to sit back, relax, and watch them do everything they've been asked to do, on their own. Independence is important in leadership, as much as teamwork is revered. You do not want to raise a leader who cannot stand on their own. Emerging leaders are not supposed to be babysit all the time; they are future babysitters and must learn the art of looking after others and doing it on their own. They must learn how to handle pressure, carry it in its heaviness, and deliver positive results under its harsh conditions. Sometimes, they would need to imagine you aren't there, and you imagining you aren't there either. This teaches self-confidence as effectively as other methods you might have on your list. When you allow emerging leaders do things and make certain decisions on their own, it gives them a sense of responsibility and trust in their own abilities. What this essentially means is that leaders must first learn to lead themselves before they are able to lead others. Michael Hyatt in his book, *Living Forward: A Proven Plan to Stop Drifting and Get the Life You Want*, made it clear that, "how we lead ourselves in life impacts how we lead those around us." While Isrealmore Ayivor, author of *The Great Hand Book of Quotes*, furthers, "Those who mistrust their own abilities are being too wicked to themselves…if you are good at discouraging yourself, you can't be a good leader, because leadership is built on inspiring others to face challenges." Too much babysitting may therefore be a shell for enclosing the potentials of emerging leaders. Giving them considerable freedom to do certain things would help you realize those that believe in themselves and those who mistrust their abilities. In the case of the latter, you will therefore need to set remedial plans in motion. Building emotional intelligence is the sixth sense of any leader; the ability to manage emotions. You must help emerging leaders realize this, as well. It is a core in leadership that extends to both the leader and members of his team. You cannot afford to have a team whose emotional wellbeing is oblivious to you. Emerging leaders must be able to tell when they, or their team members, are having a bad day. The success of any collective endeavor is an exponent of your emotional radars as a leader, which must always be active. It doesn't have to be immediately perfect. You are a leader, but human. It can be built over time, especially in your formative years as an emerging leader, by being self-aware. Followers become confident of a leader who shows a lot of care and affection towards them. Theodore Roosevelt amplifies this by saying, "No one cares how much you know, until they know how much you care." Empathy is a great asset every successful leader must possess. There is phase of project management, based on the Prince2 framework, where members of a project come together after a project, or each milestone, and discuss lessons learned from the work done. The team listens to members of the team share experiences, successes, and failures inclusive. This is not done because they just want to have a sit-down. It helps to avoid members making mistakes that have been made before. In the same vein, this means two things that can be applied in other teams. Firstly, as a leader, tell your story often, so that your followers and potential leaders get a hang of things to do when they hit a roadblock in their endeavors as leaders too. Secondly, as an emerging leader, you must be a religious listener. The experiences, good or bad, of others might serve as the light for you to become a successful leader in the future, shaping the decisions you take when you hit similar snags. It's been said several times that Rome was not built in one day. Leaders are not built in a day, as well. Mistakes will be made, and lessons will be learned. And as a leader who wants to birth another leader, it is your duty to create the best atmosphere for development. That an emerging leader didn't turn out like they were supposed to must not be your fault. However, an emerging leader in their formative years must realize, that they are ultimately responsible for the type of leaders they become. Willingness to learn and hard work and following the tips above are major ingredients for growth.

Chapter 4
101 of the Greatest Insights and Actions for Work and Life

20/20 hindsight: the "hindsight" bias or "I knew it all along phenomenon" is when you think you had the answer the whole time or that it is common sense. The problem with this is that it creates false confidence.

Try a new thing for 30 days: drop a habit, take up a new one or learn a new thing for 30 days straight. This is a great way to broaden your skills and increase your capabilities.

80% of your results are from 20% of your efforts (80/20 rule): with this rule in mind, only focus your energy on the most important things.

Make change a sense of urgency: change is not easy for many people. To get over this resistance to change, make it seem urgent.

"Absence makes the heart grow fonder" in the long-term: you will forget the negative things and only remember the positive ones.

Only absorb what works for you: you can draw inspiration from anything and anyone but only get what suits you. Tailor what you collect to fit your circumstances.

Look for the surprise: you easily remember whatever surprises you. Did you learn something that surprised you or a fact that was unexpected?

Agree and compare to create a relationship: when opinions differ, compare. Contribute when key pieces are left out by others.

Instead of telling, ask: a wandering mind is more motivated and goal-directed than that which declares its objective. Try, "will I achieve this?" instead of "I will achieve this."

MASTERING HABIT - HOW SUCCESSFUL PEOPLE THINK AND OPERATE

Ask, "how is this useful?": to make the most out of information, always ask yourself how you can use it. This helps you make insights actionable.

Ask yourself if it is effective: you may often find yourself trying things that do not work. Asking yourself if something is effective may seem simple but it can lead you to your desired results.

Learned helplessness is dangerous: when things do not go your way, watch how you give yourself an explanation. Avoid making it pervasive, personal or permanent. Questions like, "why me always?" are no good.

Balance conviction and connection: connection refers to how you connect to others while conviction refers to your rigidity or flexibility as far as your beliefs are concerned. Empathize, encourage, validate and be open to new ideas without being too accommodating.

Be-do-have rather than have-do-be; avoid holding off or having your life on wait mode. "BE" what you want, and you will "DO" according to your beliefs, leading you to "HAVE" what you want.

Careful what you wish for: the grass will always appear greener on the other side but that is not always the case.

Lead by example: this approach gives you power to act. You will not find yourself blaming others and playing victim. Set your own example of what you consider good and influence others.

Take note of specialization: specialization is great; until things change. Adaptable people get the victory in the long run.

"OCEAN" personality traits: the OCEAN (Openness, Conscientiousness, Extraversion, Agreeable and Neuroticism) refers to the Big Five framework. It is meant to understand how personality relates to behavior.

Black swan theory: some events are unpredictable but there is a way you can prepare to exploit the positive ones and persevere the negative ones.

Blink: snap judgments may tell you a lot. If correct, a little input is more useful than a lot of input. Train your senses and mind to focus on what is right and you will make great snap judgements.

Blue oceans: stop competing where there is too much competition. Look into an untapped market space if you must.

Blue zones: blue zones are the healthiest spots in the world. They teach people how to live longer lives.

Change the question, change your focus: changing your question will change your focus. Ask yourself, "what is right here?" instead of "what is wrong here?".

Change your perception or change your procedure: skillfully change your emotions. You can get over any negative emotion in a moment. You can do this by changing your solution or changing your way of experiencing it.

Change your "How" or your "Why": sometimes, the "what" is out of your control but if you change your "how" or "why" then you may achieve motivation. You will no longer depend on motivation from outside.

Begin by changing yourself: it may be difficult or impossible to change someone else but changing yourself is instant. This may include changing your views or how you do things.

Avoid "Have-To" and go for "Choose-To": choosing to do something will make it more fun. It is empowering and you will not be the victim.

Cognitive dissonance: Wikipedia defines cognitive dissonance as a discomfort brought about by having conflicting cognitions (values, beliefs, ideas) simultaneously. When one is having cognitive dissonance, one tries to change beliefs to achieve a consistent system of belief.

Delayed gratification: are you "present-oriented" or "future-oriented"? A future-oriented person delays gratification and according to research, navigates through life better.

Deliberate practice: Malcolm Gladwell, the author of *Outliers: The Story of Success*, says that to be successful, you must practice the task for about 10,000 hours. You become experienced by repetitively practicing a skill, tracking your performance, assessing your effectiveness and listening to feedback.

Delphi method: this technique involves using experts to predict and forecast information. A facilitator asks experts to give answers to specific questions anonymously. The collective answers are then used to conclude.

Do it daily: to get into a new habit or get out of an old one, you need to do it daily. Create a habit and condition yourself to do it.

Causational vs. correlational: when two things happen simultaneously, it does not necessary mean that one caused the other. They may just be correlated. Knowing the difference will make you better suited to get to the root cause.

Stop waiting for inspiration: begin by acting, motivation will come.

Doublethink: learn to think twice. Focus on both the negative and the positive. When you imagine the two sides, you can visualize effectively.

Dream big dreams: small dreams are not very inspirational. Big ones stir your blood and inspire your mind.

Emotional intelligence: EQ may hold you back or propel you forward. It is defined as the ability to point out, analyze and control your emotions and that of others.

Energized differentiation: be different with vision, dynamism and invention.

Enjoy the journey: take a moment to smell the roses. Come up with ways to have fun in your journey. Sometimes, your journey is all you have.

Errors in value and errors in odds: according to Dan Gilbert, people make poor choices because they fail to estimate odds well and they are also not good when it comes to estimating value.

Relationship before influence: a relationship helps you know the concerns and needs of the other party. It also builds trust.

The third alternative: do not get into a win-lose situation. Find another option because it is always there.

A first impression is a lasting impression: you only get one chance to create a first impression. If you blow your chance, you can change their perception. Let the other person assess you in a new context or situation.

Fortune cookie effect: you can rationalize whatever you want in your mind. You take actions that cause something to come true.

What you can control over what you cannot: not everything is under your control and this should not be a reason for you to give up. Control your actions, attitude, approach and response.

Gambler's fallacy: just because an action or event has not taken place for some time, does not mean that its chances of happening now are high.

Groupthink: two heads are better than one—this statement is not always true. A group may exaggerate decisions, making the final decision too conservative or too risky.

Remove the unessential: according to Bruce Lee, it is daily decrease over daily increase.

Halo effect: sometimes you assess someone globally and apply that to a specific trait. For instance, you may think someone is likeable and, consequently, assume that they are friendly and intelligent.

The end of the story: the ending of a story is more important than its beginning.

Measure your life: the best way to measure life is regarding the number of people you touch.

Informational power: information is an impermanent form of power and holding on to it is an even weaker form of power.

Evaluate your thinking: everyone's mind is flawed. Your thinking has traps and pitfalls. Challenge your thinking and eliminate poor thinking patterns.

Extrinsic motivation vs intrinsic motivation: find out what motivates and drives you. Do this by connecting your job to your values.

MASTERING HABIT - HOW SUCCESSFUL PEOPLE THINK AND OPERATE

Irrationality: always treat each decision as crucial if you are looking to make a change.

Energy management over time management: everyone has 24 hours in a day. The only thing that is under your control is energy. If you manage your energy, you will do more with less effort.

Jigsaw technique: if you want people to overcome their prejudice, pair them up. They will realize, as they work on the project, that they are all humans with vulnerabilities, feelings and basic needs.

Job satisfaction: to make your job more enjoyable, focus on feedback, autonomy, task significance, task identity and skill variety.

Johari window: know yourself and show yourself. This way, you will find it easier to share information that matters and enhance communication.

Learning style: is your learning style kinesthetic, visual or audio?

Less is more: less here refers to more focus.

Linchpin: work towards being indispensable. One way to do this is to always go above the call of duty. Give your all, do more art and break rules to tweak the game.

Link to good feelings: a new habit will be easier to adopt if it is linked to good feelings. You can barely do things that do not feel good. Reframe the meaning of the action.

Maslow's hierarchy of needs: Maslow suggested that there is a set of needs commonly shared by people. Understanding this concept will help you know more about what drives you and others.

Mentors are short-cuts: with a good mentor, you will avoid pitfalls. A good mentor shows you what you should focus on and hasten your journey to success.

Micro-expressions: this is a very quick involuntary facial expression. It is hard to hide this type of expressions, regardless of how much you know about them.

Mindstyle: do you prefer sequential, random, concrete or abstract? Understand how you prefer to grasp information and order it.

Mirror cells: everyone has mirror neurons that mirror the feelings or intentions of other people. They can help you explain empathy and imitation.

Flexible people are favored by nature: survival is not for the most intelligent or the strongest, it is for those that adapt very well to change.

Similarities bind; it is true that opposites attract but people attain a special connection at the values. Shared values bring people together.

Parkinson's law: assign less time to something if you want it to be done faster. Work will expand to fill the available time.

Pygmalion effect: what you expect is what you get.

Reciprocity of liking: people like those that like them. If you do not like yourself, you will not like the people that like you.

Return on luck: Jim Collins suggests leveraging luck by seeing it as an event rather than an indefinable aura. Aim at achieving a high return on luck (ROL).

Satisfice: to make decisions faster, experts satisfice. They look for the first solution that is perfect for that situation.

Self-efficacy: one's self-efficacy beliefs will determine a person's behavior, motivation and thoughts.

Dispositional vs situational: did the situation cause you to do that or is it just who you are?

Get small, think big: small is a key to flexibility, increased effectiveness and more efficiency.

Social loafing: when people are more, they work less hard. People put in less effort when they are working in groups.

Speak to the communication needs of people: communication needs include appreciation, approval, accuracy and action. People will give you clues on what they need to hear.

Start with why: you should communicate, act and think in the same way. Start with the thought, from the inside out. Begin with why, then how and finally what.

MASTERING HABIT - HOW SUCCESSFUL PEOPLE THINK AND OPERATE

Synthetic happiness: learn to create your own happiness; it is just as good as genuine happiness.

The effort effect: effort is what makes a difference, not talent. Your effort, in turn, is facilitated or limited by your mindset. Another thing: reward your efforts.

The long view: you cannot predict what will happen in the future. You can, however, play the "What-Ifs". Use forecasting to prepare for what may happen.

The paradox of choice: the more choices you make, the poorer your decision will be. You may not even be able to make the decision.

The power of identity; be rooted in something that will last while enjoying your growth journey at the same time.

The power of regrets: if you reflect on your worst, you will be motivated to unleash your best.

The principle of contrast: you can easily lose perspective. Compare with something worse. This principle of contrast is useful when changing perspective, explaining value or negotiating fees.

The progress principle: small progress can significantly make your day. Perfection is not what matters, progress is.

The "Good Life" secret: learn to allocate more time to your values. Ask yourself how you can do more of the things you love at work.

The two happiness questions: "How happy are you with your life?" and "How happy are you?".

Thoughts that work for you: think thoughts that will serve you better.

"To-Date" vs. "To-Go": if you commit yourself to a goal, you will focus on what is left (and will be more motivated). If you are not that committed, you will concentrate on how much you have accomplished.

Important vs Urgent: you will achieve your long-term goals if you spend time on the important but non-urgent matters.

Befriend stress: anxiety is a cognitive response while stress is a fight-or-flight response. Stress can be useful while performing physical tasks or simple tasks.

Willpower is like a muscle: you can strengthen willpower through practice, just like a muscle. Know that you can also fatigue it; it is limited.

Yerkes-Dodson human performance curve: do not stress yourself beyond your capacity. You will start producing less with more effort.

You are the company you keep; friends can help you grow or hold you back. They will influence your actions, emotions, attitude and thoughts.

Your strengths facilitate your growth: focus on your strengths if you want to accelerate your success.

Thoughts shape feelings: shift your focus to change your feelings.

Zeigarnik effect: to overcome procrastination, convince yourself to do something for "just a few minutes". You will be motivated to finish what you have already began.

"Some people dream of success, while others wake up and work hard at it."

-Napoleon Hill

Chapter 5
The Secret to Living a Fulfilling Life

Everyone wants a full, satisfied life. Many people do not necessarily want a long life; just a fulfilling one characterized by happiness, achievements, and zero regrets. However, this seems like a fantasy to many. People around you may throw some discouraging comments your way, saying how a 'fulfilling life' is for the rich. While that may be partially true, you will be relieved to know that financial freedom is not necessary for a full life. Living a life of fullness begins with a willingness to learn. Every working professional remembers the time when they were in school. The morning lecturers and the exams were not so fun, were they? You wished to be done with it and begin working. Now that you are working, there are days when you miss being in school. College life may not be very stressing compared to your current life. There is a lot that you need to experience and learn. With your social life, business, family commitments an everything else, time is a limited resource. You must find new ways, every time, to absorb new stuff efficiently. When you gain new knowledge and learn new skills, you get solutions and answers to your life problems and in turn, a higher sense of fulfillment. Formal education and qualifications are important if you want to secure a good job. However, going to school is not the only type of learning there is. You learn in many ways and the experiences help you grow. You can acquire knowledge and develop skill sets anywhere. Nonetheless, lifelong learning involves having a positive attitude towards learning, both for professional and personal development. A lifelong learner develops and learns because they have made a choice to do just that; it is a voluntary and deliberate act. When you become a lifelong learner, your understanding of the world is enhanced, your quality of life improved and you can access better opportunities. People are now retiring later in life, thanks to increased life expectancy. As a lifelong learner, you have better chances of having productive working days. You will experience profound progress and a sense of wellbeing. A knowledgeable and highly skilled employee is considered an asset in a company. This means faster promotion and, of course, a salary increase. With more expertise, a worker adds value to customers as well as employers. Expertise is also considered a major quality of effective leaders. When you keep on amassing knowledge, you will have an advantage over those that do not think lifelong learning is important. People change career paths all the time. You can always start afresh in life, no matter how old you are. When you educate yourself and learn new things, your opportunities widen. You will have a way out if what you are currently doing is not fulfilling.

Chapter 6
Goals in Life

Richard Feynman was a physicist who won a Nobel Prize for quantum electrodynamics. However, there is something about him that many people have no clue about: he was a safecracker, a good one. One time while he was in the New Mexico Desert in 1940, Feynman got bored. He was focusing on the Manhattan project which birthed the atomic bomb. He decided to have some fun by pranking his colleagues. He knew that many of them were not careful when dealing with top secret document safes. Feynman started leaving them notes such as: "I borrowed document no. LA4312 – Feynman the safecracker." He became very good at these pranks and the Colonel in charge advised the people to change their lock combination if Feynman came anywhere near the safe. Feynman tells this and many more of his stories in his autobiography: *Surely, You're Joking Mr. Feynman!* One of the most admirable things about Feynman is his deep curiosity on things, such that he only committed himself to that which he found interesting. Obviously, he was a focused person; however, he was guided by an orienting impulse that was beyond simple ambitions and goals. He was interested in going past the known. Goals are common in just about every pursuit. People look ahead, try to predict what may give them a happy future and then narrow down to a specific thing. What if that is the wrong way? Is the Answer Living Goal to Goal? An orientation is necessary when you are dealing with the future. If you do not have one, you will be shaped completely by randomness and luck. Goal setting is taught very early on in life so people can keep up. Later, when you join corporations, you find even more goals, encouraging the tendency.

Whether you are setting personal or SMART goals, without a framework or with a framework, they are all common in that they are concrete. Goals are important and having one may be better than having none. Some people are genetically predisposed to be more satisfied in in an accomplishment than others. However, living goal to goal can be problematic. First, it tries to predict the future which is unpredictable. Life changes, you change. Second, it builds an anchor. Your expectations of contentment and happiness are bound on a singular thing and you may forget other joyful experiences. The solution? The pursuit of interestingness solves the problem of goal setting. It is nebulous and vague enough to honestly consider the unpredictability of the future but keeps you from getting lost in randomness and pure luck. Interestingness is taking on a random project because it might teach you something new about yourself. It is viewing someone you just met as an individual who might lead you to new dimensions and not as a potential partner or ladder to something. If interestingness becomes your goal, your actual goals become fluid. The best things in life come randomly, not when you are striving for virtual perfection. SMART goal setting is an efficient method trusted by high achievers. Perhaps, there is something you have always wanted to achieve but you just cannot seem to be successful. If you do not approach your goals with seriousness and a great attitude, you will barely achieve them. SMART goal setting is your key to get to where you have always wanted to go. This is a method of setting goals that takes into consideration certain factors about the goal relative to whoever is setting it. The factors are the five letters in the acronym. The goal setting is relative to the specific goal setter because people are different. This is what the acronym stands for:

S – Specific
M – Measurable
A - Achievable
R – Realistic
T – Time bound

What is so special about this goal setting metric?

The Long-Lasting Impact of SMART Goals

SMART goal setting is partially responsible for the success of people such as Steve Jobs and Stephen Cooley. Here are the impacts of SMART goal setting: Clear your goals: this goal setting method allows you to understand all the phases of the goal. You will always be asking the relevant questions as far as your goal is concerned. Motivates you: SMART goal setting breaks down your goal into smaller ones or milestones. This makes the bigger goal appear less intimidating. Saves time: when you have a strategy, you are likely to achieve more. Being strategic means that your goal is SMART. If you look at your goals and you cannot see any of these features (specific, measurable, achievable, realistic, and time bound), know that you may not go far. You become more motivated when you write down your goals. Enhances self-discipline: everyone should try self-improvement regularly. Setting SMART goals will help you realize that effort is required on your side to achieve them. Specific: vague goals are not advisable. You may not even realize when you have achieved them. For instance, a goal like "start planning for retirement" is not specific. Go ahead and outline how exactly you plan on preparing. A specific goal has clear components and it will be easier to work towards. Measurable: a goal such as "save millions of dollars for retirement" is not measurable. It would be better to set a goal for saving a specific amount every month towards retirement. Achievable: is your goal actionable? You must resonate with your goal. Make sure you have the resources (not necessarily all of them) to achieve the goal. The time frame is also an important factor to consider. Realistic: are you willing to sacrifice all that is required to achieve your goal? Time bound, you must write the start and end date of you goal. Once you have done that, break down the goal into milestones, chunks, or phases. Deadlines will motivate you to act. Over to you now. Go for your dreams. What is a meaningful and fulfilling life? There are tons of answers to this question on the internet. They may all seem to be great ideas, but they are directionless and vague. A better answer would be a list of goals to lead you to a fulfilling life.

These goals are divided into four categories:
1 - 8: concentrate on long-term happiness
9 -15: nurture deep relationships
16 - 23: tap into your potential
24 - 29: live a life driven by purpose

1. A gratitude journal: this basically means writing down four things that you are grateful for every morning.
2. Make a life plan: a detailed life plan will give you an idea of where you want to be and what you want to achieve.
3. A healthy exercise routine: exercise boosts energy levels, your mood, health, happiness, and much more.
4. Give back: not only does volunteering improve happiness, but it is also fulfilling.
5. A creative hobby: everyone has an innate creative ability. Look for a way to express yours.
6. Become mindful: teach yourself to live in the moment.
7. Be kind: share kindness with strangers even when you do not feel like it.
8. Pursue personal growth: you cannot live a fulfilling life unless you grow as a person.
9. Get away from bad relationships: only focus on the relationships that matter; not those that drain you.
10. Be with people you admire you will become like the people you surround yourself with.
11. Routine phone calls: set a regular reminder to call your loved ones.
12. Something new once a month: if you are trying to be closer to someone (spouse or friend), find a new activity to do together every month.
13. Volunteer together: volunteer with your loved ones regularly.

14. Deep, vulnerable conversations: being vulnerable builds trust and deepens relationships.
15. Do not talk about yourself for one evening: this will help you learn more about someone else.
16. Do something scary: try doing something that you fear.
17. Take a risk: this could mean starting a business.
18. Personal development books: these books teach you so much about yourself and the world.
19. Get more responsibility: ask your boss for greater responsibilities.
20. Find a mentor: mentorship is powerful, and you will get to higher levels.
21. Mentor someone: you will learn so much as you teach.
22. Embrace failure: take failures as an opportunity to learn.
23. Know yourself: what are your weaknesses, strengths and personality type?
24. Discover your dreams: set time to imagine your future and do not hold back.
25. Define your values: know what matters and focus on that.
26. Be authentic: be true to yourself every day.
27. Try new things: explore and seek excitement.
28. Pursue your dream career: apply tirelessly for your dream job.
29. Defend your dream: do not take your eyes off your goals. Say "no" if you must.

Chapter 7
Learning from Failure

It is said that failure is an amazing teacher. But if that is the case, why are so many people unable to gain knowledge from this supposedly "great teacher"? Why do people keep failing? The issue is that, although failure is an amazing teacher, it is a cryptic one too. It is not easy to understand its lessons, especially when you are still lost in demoralization, disappointment, frustration, and nursing your bruised ego. Sometimes failure also comes with hopelessness, resentment and embarrassment. To benefit from your failure, you need to find a way to decipher the "teachable moments" that are hidden tactfully within failure. You need a method to help you understand what the lessons are and how you can use them to improve your chances of a successful future. The guidelines below will enable you to assess your failures and find the specific issues that you must correct as you pursue goals. You will need to do a lot of soul searching and thinking so do not hesitate to take time to recover from the punch of a new failure before you start. Reevaluate your planning: how long did it take you to plan the best way to attain your goal before you began? Did you think about the problems or hurdles that you might face and how you would overcome them? A big number of people barely spend time planning things like these even though unexpected obstacles are part of life. In future, have a general strategy, think about potential setbacks and find a way to overcome them beforehand. Reevaluate your preparation: this step is a very crucial one but still, many people skip it. For instance, think about someone who aspires to live a healthy life by joining a gym and attending twice a week. This plan can be easily shattered if the babysitter cancels last minute and she has no alternative. If she prepared a backup plan for childcare, she would be able to attend gym more consistently and slide into the habit. Another example is when someone begins a diet but does not get rid of unhealthy foods in the house to replace them with healthy ones. When planning future goals, take measures that will increase your chances of success. Reevaluate your execution: were your efforts consistent? Were you lacking motivation and lagging in your work ethic? Go back and analyze when and why your efforts dropped. Understand what circumstances led to the derailment of your efforts and know how you will address them should they occur in the future. Focus on the variables within your control: it is normal for failure to make you feel helpless and passive, leading you to believe that you may never succeed even if you try. However, understand that these feelings are perceptual distortions. You have more control over situations than you realize. There is always something you can do to improve a situation such as being more knowledgeable, improving your network, or building relationships with potential clients.

"MOST GREAT PEOPLE HAVE achieved their greatest success just one step beyond their greatest failure."
-Napoleon Hill

Chapter 8
Create the Future You Visualize

Change is reinvention. Whenever a big shift occurs in your life (such as a relationship, leaving a job, moving, or losing a loved one), you must choose who you want to become. Otherwise, you risk never achieving your potential. Many adults have reinvented themselves several times in their lives. However, what many people forget is that you must chose reinvention. Every time you do it, you forge a new path for yourself, intentionally and with foresight. When you wait for your future to find you, you will wait in vain. You will be lost in sadness and confusion or find yourself in a situation that you do not want. When you've been struggling in a bad situation for a while, one day you will realize that part of the reason you have been stuck is that you have no idea where you want to go; you have no end goal. This happens when you're thinking about your past and not your future.

Here are a few steps you can use you to reinvent yourself.

1. Have A Vision For Your Future

Find a quiet place and sit with your eyes closed. Imagine all the people, situations and places that you know you must leave behind. Next, imagine your ideal future; it could be a group of people, a feeling or even a situation—such as a great job. Imagine how you would feel being in that new place. Imagine the sun rising behind your future and it's warm glow lighting your face. Take a moment to stand and quietly voice your gratefulness for all the things that came before. After thanking the past, look towards the sun, with appreciation and compassion, picture yourself walking away from it and into your future.

1. Write About Your Reinvention

Picture a scene from your reinvention or write about how you want it to play out. Where do you see yourself living? What is your morning, afternoon and evening routine? How do you spend your days and who are your friends? Keep writing until the excitement of the exercise wears out. Write everything from scenes, to dialogues to plans. Keep the writing safe and look at it every now and then.

1. Surround Yourself with Things That Remind You of Your Ideal Life

If you desire a job in a certain field, put images or objects from that place where you can see them daily. If it is a home, get a picture of the house of your choice and place it near your door. Whatever it is, let it be something that reminds you of where you want to be.

1. Break Up Your Vision into Workable Tasks

What do you do daily to create your vision? Find new friends? Look for a job? Be specific. Create a list and a schedule of everything that you need to do. Commit yourself and do it, one day at a time.

1. Envision Yourself Walking to Your Future Every Day

Each morning or evening, imagine yourself moving towards the rising sun and all your dreams. Remind yourself why you must do this.

Chapter 9
Innovation Personalities: Which One Are You?

Personalities for leaders are divided into four groups; Reactionary, Traditional, Evolutionary, and Revolutionary. As a leader, read through and figure out where you belong. Think about your organization and your team too. Where do they fall? Armed with that knowledge, you will have an idea of how you can all work together to achieve the innovation and change that is needed. Revolutionaries are dedicated to innovation. They are thrilled to know they serve a purpose bigger than themselves. An Evolutionary has the potential of becoming a Revolutionary. Innovation is all about serving people, solving their problems, and enhancing their lives. It is neither a talent nor a static skill. It is a set of processes, tools, and skills that you choose to gain, practice, and maintain. Anyone can access it. You only need to know where you lie now and what you want to be.

Revolutionary

Different sources give you different tags—Innovator, Provocateur, Disruptor, Reinventor. You revolutionize processes. You think designs; that is, your mind works like that of a designer. New ideas energize you and you can be described as curious, open-minded, and positive. For you, change is not a challenge but an opportunity. You make use of an iterative process and design tools to find solutions. You are committed to being close to your customer. That is how you make sure that you are asking the right questions. With this approach, you co-design together with customers. Through journey mapping, you uncover the hidden needs of your customers, and experiment with solutions using prototyping. Constraints do not scare you and instead, you milk the benefits out of them.

Evolutionary

You love to bring change, but you are cautious. Change is only comfortable for you if it is incremental. Some Evolutionaries are Revolutionaries who were hurt by market forces causing them to lose some courage. Others aspire to be Revolutionaries and they are trying to gather experience. One expert advises that you must be less concerned about being perfect. Venture out of your comfort zone and dare to cultivate a relationship with your customers. Try to experiment a little more and co-design with your customers.

Traditionalists

As a Traditionalist, you are comfortable with your solution. You are fine with it. You will say your customers are happy if someone asks you. However, in your "heart of hearts" you know that you have drifted further away from your users. Fortunately, there are ways through which you can nurture empathy and grow closer to them. Change your mindset from product-centered to experience-centered and you will have courage to have a unique vision.

Reactionary

Change is not fun for you and you tend to reject new ideas. The fear of the unknown causes you to make excuses as to why you cannot implement new concepts. You know, deep down, that experimentation and agility make organizations evolve. Learn to think like a designer—try to see the good that this will do to your organization.

Chapter 10
Self-Doubt

It happens to everyone. Sometimes, you question yourself and wonder if you are doing well or if you can face whatever comes your way. You doubt yourself when making choices and decisions or feel "not good enough". That is self-doubt. It is when you are not feeling capable or confident when performing a task. Self-doubt is not always bad. However, when it becomes persistent and mixed with fear, it can negatively affect your life. Suppose your boss assigns an important task to you because he trusts your capabilities. Instead of being proud that he has recognized your efforts, you panic. You start wondering whether you will do a great job, or you will make a fool out of yourself. You stress over each decision you must make and imagine everything that may go wrong. This fear will start playing a huge role and introduce you to another friend, procrastination. You will be demotivated and keep off doing the work as much as possible. Eventually, you hand in the last-minute work feeling that you would have done better.

5 Causes of Self Doubt

Past Mistakes and Experiences

Bad experiences in your past can affect your present reactions. They can shake your beliefs. You should know that your past is a closed case and there is nothing you can change about it. Do not reference past experiences unless you are learning from them. Your upbringing shapes your personality and habits. If your parents constantly told you that you do not measure up, you probably question yourself a lot. Remind yourself that you are now a grown up. It is your life and you can decide what is best for you. There is so much competition in the world and you will constantly catch yourself comparing. Social media does not make this any easier. It is easy to envy other people and feel like you are not doing well enough. Comparing is not that bad if you are doing it to improve yourself. Appreciate yourself. New challenges bring about feelings of insecurity and uncertainty. Take this challenge as an opportunity to learn instead of feeling incapable. Tell yourself that mistakes are allowed. Previous success may bring about fear because you wonder if you can do as well as you did back then. Do not focus on replicating past success; think about outperforming it.

Overcoming Self Doubt

- Focus on the present moment and the positive aspects.
- Take a break and boost your optimism.
- Seek help when necessary.

21-Day Challenge to Gain Self-Confidence

This is about noting things down. Day 1 to 7: write three things that you are thankful for every morning. Day 8 to 14: in addition to the above, note the times you feel insecure and the reason for that. Day 15 to 21: write down what you did to overcome the uncomfortable feelings.

Chapter 11
Ambition VS. Talent

Ambition overrides resources and talents as far as the pursuit for success is concerned. When someone has an ambitious attitude, they can attain satisfaction and triumph, regardless of the obstacles that come their way. If you have the courage, the dream and the will to move forward, you will go far in life. If you lack the ambition to work your ass off any time, your talent will be pretty much useless. There are countless people all over the world who are a waste of potential and ability. Most of the people with an elite status were mere underdogs. They were ambitious to prove everyone else wrong instead of proving them right and ending up as a nobody. When someone is fueled by ambition, they make sacrifices and work hard to attain the life they have always dreamt of—and they always succeed. They are in love with the passionate and determined person they are becoming and the fulfillment they get from their work. This is their reason to continue believing in themselves and never give up. Ambition gives people a purpose in life, it leads them to fight for what they truly believe in. Society often views heavy ambition as a negative thing because most people think that it is an addiction to power or a characteristic for greed. This is not it, however. It is just a strong desire to get away from mediocrity. People hate power and greed because they do not have the courage to explore where their ambition may take them. Ambitious people know that shortcuts do not exist. The only way to get where they want is persistence. They never ignore a single instance of drive because this is what gets them closer to where they are going. Before you set out to achieve your goals, you will have them focused on something. When you lack a strong motivation and ambition to win, you will not have a very high chance of winning because you will not be moved to give it your all. If you are ambitious, however, you will do whatever it takes, go beyond your limits and keep at it until you achieve greatness. Always be together with your ambition; be on the same page and understand one another. Are you prepared to give anything up to accomplish your goals in the next 10 years? Write down what you are willing to sacrifice; be it parties, vacations, or anything else. Simply wanting to be rich cannot lead you to achieve your goals. You must work harder than most people. To realize all your goals, you must want them—much like your desire to breathe. Being lazy should not even cross your mind. You will have highs and lows. That is part of the journey. Follow your dreams and embrace your passion. Allow your ambition to fuel you.

Chapter 12
Take 100% Responsibility for Your Life

Napoleon Hill talks about his "other self" in his book, *Outwitting the Devil*. This side of him was not unclear or indecisive about the future. It completely operated out of definiteness of purpose and faith. Hill went through deep depression for several months and he sunk to rock bottom. At one point, he decided that enough was enough. He decided to follow his "other self" with total obedience, even when it seemed crazy. According to certain research conducted at Yale University, if you hesitate even for several seconds, your chances of doing what you were feeling inspired to do drops dramatically. Always act immediately whenever you are inspired to carry out an action. Every second is important. Hill decided to act immediately and completely disregard his other self.

A Life Without Hesitation

Hill's voice advised him to ask for financial assistance in publishing his books. It gave him amazing business ideas. Napoleon Hill is not the only one who has experienced this "other self" concept. Tony Robbins talks about it as a 3-part process:

- Decide while you are in a peak or passionate state.

- Commit to your decision by setting up several accountability mechanisms and removing conflicting things in your environment.

- Resolve to finish what you have started.

Big Decisions in a Peak State

If your decisions are not made in a peak state, they will be small-minded and weak.

Having yourself in a peak state is your responsibility, every single day. Avoid dragging yourself through life. Set new standards for the day and for your life. What Does Commitment Mean? To commit to something means that you will carry it out to completion. You have no escape routes and you burn any bridges that may lead to distraction. Once you have decided, you do not turn back.

Resolving That the Decision Is Final

When you resolve something within yourself, it means that it is done inside you, before it is done. Once you have decided that something is done, you will achieve it—no matter what comes your way.

Many People Want Certainty

People will often forsake inner freedom for external security. However, when an individual has inner freedom, they have no problem embracing the uncertainty that comes with pursuing their dreams. You already know what you want, and you will make sure you get it. You have faith that God will help you.

Resolve Means Knowing That You Will Achieve Your Goals

The moment you have made a resolve, you know it will happen. Every day, you wake up with more faith and reassure yourself that your dreams will come true. Nothing can stand in your way.

Not Many People Have Confidence

People break the commitments they have made to themselves every other day and they, therefore, have no genuine confidence. Confidence cannot be faked; it shows how you relate to yourself.

Challenge

If you are feeling inspired to do something today or to do more, decide and commit to it.

"TELL ME HOW YOU USE your spare time, and how you spend your money, and I will tell you where and what you will be in ten years from now."

-Napoleon Hill

Chapter 13
Self-Care

Do you regularly do something nice for yourself? A lot of people falsely believe that self-care only involves enjoyment and indulgence. The truth is that it goes beyond that. It is all about understanding your mind, body, and respecting its limits. It is about taking care of yourself in a holistic way. Going on a vegan diet, meditating, or any other extreme measures are not quite necessary in self-care. The point is to do things that are in your best interest. How do you do that? The methods below are tried and tested. They will lead you to an overall better place and help you live a great life.

Listen to Yourself

Self-care is generally about knowing yourself. Be in tune with your thoughts, emotions, and feelings, in addition to knowing your limitations.

Who are you and what is your purpose?

Do the roles that you play at your job, home, and society fulfill that purpose? Whatever you are chasing should be meaningful to you. Figuring out your purpose leads you to know what you want to do and why you want to do it.

Continual Education

Lifelong learning is a part of self-care.

It is practical: in the past, acquiring knowledge required a lot of effort. Today, things are different. You have the internet and you can learn as many skills as you want without leaving your home. It boosts your confidence: learning makes you move beyond your comfort zone and make you more confident. You will also expose yourself to many perspectives and ideas—which may lead to better connections with other people. It opens more opportunities: the economy is ever changing. The more flexible you are, the more opportunities you will have. It will be hard for you to be unemployed. A highly skilled and knowledgeable person is indispensable.

Improve Your Habits

This is the last piece is this self-care regimen. Habits define you. They are created over time. A good example of this is "you are what you eat". If you are always eating healthy and nourishing foods, your body will be healthier. With good habits, you will attain your goals: your habits dictate your life (day and night). They determine when you wake up and when you get to work and even whether you brush your teeth before bed. Believe it or not, your habits may cause you to achieve your goals or fail. If your habits push you towards your goals, your days are purposeful.

Habits prioritize your time: what takes up your free time? Nobody can say that they do not waste time during their day. However, if you pursue good habits, you can set a healthy pattern for spending your time.

Your Well Being Is Your First Priority

The modern life is a very busy one. If you care for yourself first, it will be easier to care for everything and everyone else. You cannot take care of others when you are in a poor state of mind.

"OUR ONLY LIMITATIONS are those we set up in our minds."
   -Napoleon Hill

Chapter 14
Turn Stress into Success

Multitudes of people have faced stress deeply, and some of them have successfully overcome it. Stress negatively affects a person's well-being and when it goes on for long periods of time, it could lead to sleep problems, coronary diseases, depression, and anxiety. What Causes Stress? Stress is like a reaction to a threat. In ancient times, it helped with survival by triggering 'flight' or 'fight' response. In current times, it helps in the management of emotional and mental overwhelm. Because some of these problems occur daily, many people can barely find the mind space and emotional strength to respond properly every day. Stress symptoms can either be deeply buried or obvious. Stress will often manifest as mental, emotional, and physical discomfort. Physical signs such as sleeplessness, upset stomach, tiredness and headaches. Mental signs are inability to switch off or enjoy oneself, the feeling of being down, or feeling overwhelmed. Emotional signs are such as feeling trapped, loneliness, depression, nervousness, anxiety, impatience, and irritability. Overeating/emotional eating: food triggers your brain reward system and makes you feel better for a moment. You may overeat to numb your feelings. Reliance on alcohol or any other substance: this helps you relax for a short time. However, if you keep doing it you may get addicted. Nervous behaviors: these may include pinching your skin or chewing your nails to release nervous energy. Procrastination: in the end, this one only increases anxiety and makes you feel worse about yourself. Passive aggressiveness: when you are too stressed, you will want to be alone. You will barely have the patience for other people. Rumination: focusing on negative stressors will have you asking so many questions and brooding over your circumstances. Chronic illnesses: research has shown that stress largely contributes to the development of conditions such as Ulcerative Colitis, Crohn's and IBS.

Part A: Establish the 4 Causes of Stress

Stress is a threat, as mentioned above. In the modern world, the threats can come in four dimensions. The first step is to know your biggest stressor. Safety Threats: Everyone wants to be safe in terms of a stable job, financial freedom, and good health. What is stressing you—health issues, financial freedom, or work pressure? Love and belonging threats: a sense of belonging, intimacy, and love are important. Is the lack of these things stressing you? Self-esteem threats: is your self-esteem being affected? Where are you seeking validation from? Self-actualization threat: are you fulfilling your potential? Are you living your best life?

Part B: Change Your Mindset

Use your thinking brain rather than your primitive brain. Your thinking brain does not respond unconsciously; it makes logical choices.

Let the stress push you to be better.

Part C: Manage the Stress

- Do not avoid it, accept it.
- Be proactive in changing your situation.
- Practice the "circle of influence" concept.
- Develop grit.

"A POSITIVE MIND FINDS a way it can be done; A negative mind looks for all the ways it can't be done."

-Napoleon Hill

Chapter 15
How Successful People Think and Operate

Successful people do not see the world like everyone else. It is not because they are perfect or because their version of life is easier than yours. However, in one way or another, they always appear to bounce ahead. It does not matter the obstacles they face, the problems that come their way, or how loud their critics sneer—they always come up with a way to emerge victorious. How do they do this? They have a few beliefs that they hold on to. These beliefs make a difference in the way they fight for success. They do not view the beliefs as some random motivational quotes from a book. What they believe in impacts every aspect of their daily life.

These Are 18 Things That Successful People Believe

1. Everything is possible if you are prepared to put in enough effort and time.
2. If you make up excuses to get out of doing something, that 'something' is exactly what you are supposed to be doing.
3. The people who do not like you much are the ones that will give you the most truthful advice.
4. Whoever wants something the most is the one who will eventually win it.
5. Whatever it takes is exactly what it takes to achieve your life desires.
6. If you want to keep losing, surround yourself with negative people.

7. Gratitude, action, fear, and worry are choices that you make.
8. If you are not prepared to master all the details, you have very slim chances of winning.
9. Apathy is a hindrance to achieving something fantastic.
10. Just because you failed last time does not mean that you should stop trying.
11. It does not matter how bad you have it; if you want to make, you will.
12. No one is responsible for making your decisions. You get to make all your decisions.
13. If you have been yearning for a second chance, today is your second chance; make use of it.
14. Your effort's intensity determines how fast you progress
15. Be prepared to listen and acquire knowledge; otherwise, you will never get better.
16. Your actions in private determine your course of development.
17. Just because your critics are loud is not reason to believe that they are on the right.
18. If a solution is easy, guaranteed and fast, it will probably not be useful in the long run.

In Their Heart of Hearts, Winners Believe That Nothing Is Impossible

In most cases, they have no idea how they are going to win. But even then, they truly believe that they are going to find a way. According to them, the great equalizer is effort. When they have no idea what they should do, they take time to learn and even perfect it. The things you believe will bring change in your life. This is a good time to pause and seriously think about what motivates you. What are your beliefs? Do you think that life is not fair? Do you constantly believe that you have it harder than everyone else? Do you blame everyone but yourself?

"SET YOUR MIND ON A definite goal and observe how quickly the world stands aside to let you pass."
    -Napoleon Hill

Chapter 16
Habits of Rich People

These habits define rich people. If you adopt the habits below, you will be on the path to a wealthy life as well.

Junk Food

Unless you feed yourself properly, you will not feel well and, in turn, you cannot think well. Focus on healthy fats, protein, vegetables, and fruit.

Gambling

The lottery is otherwise known as the Fool's Tax. You can never become rich if you use a significant amount of your income for gambling.

Singular Goals

Wealthy people set a single clear goal and set out to achieve it.

Exercise

Exercising and eating well go hand in hand. Exercising boosts your energy and mood. Find something you enjoy like walking or running.

Audio Books

When you are taking a walk or commuting to work, listen to educational or inspirational audios —feed your brain.

To-Do List

Before you go to sleep, create a to-do list for the following day, even for small things. When you cross them off you will feel motivated!

Non-Fiction

To enjoy non-fiction books, look for subjects that you find interesting.

Volunteer

Volunteering increases happiness. Another thing, you can make valuable connections while volunteering which may prove helpful in future.

Happy Birthday!

People with close social relationships tend to be happier. The happier you are, the more successful you are likely to be. When you remember your loved ones' birthdays, you foster the relationships.

Write Goals Down

Writing your goals down increases your chances of achieving them. When something is written down, it remains at the forefront of your mind.

Read

Reading should be a part of you. Find books that teach you something.

Bite Your Tongue

Learn to pick your battles. You do not have to speak your mind every time. Sometimes you must be quiet even when someone is being difficult.

Network

Who you know matters! Your next big job can come from anywhere. Attend Meetups and industry events.

TV

There is almost nothing good about watching TV. Instead of wasting time, do something beneficial such as visiting a friend, reading a book, or making a healthy meal.

Reality TV

Watching TV can be justified but watching reality TV is just dumb. This cannot be said nicely. If you watch reality TV, you need to be better.

Wake Early

Early hours are quiet and peaceful. Use this time to be productive because you have no one to interrupt you. Waking up early also allows you to start your day calmly.

Teach Habits

MASTERING HABIT - HOW SUCCESSFUL PEOPLE THINK AND OPERATE

This is more about adopting good habits so your children can copy them and less about teaching them.

Opportunities

Many wealthy people believe that if you have good habits, you will have better opportunities.

Bad Luck

When you foster bad habits, be prepared for bad outcomes. For instance, failure to floss may lead to gum disease and, in turn, expensive dental work.

Be Learning, Always

Never stop learning. Take a dancing class, learn new skills—just learn something.

Love to Read

The importance of reading cannot be emphasized enough.

Many successful people will tell you that reading has partially contributed to their success. Before Elon Musk became Tesla CEO, he read for 10 hours every day. Bill Gates, Microsoft CEO, completes one book every week.

Warren Buffett

Buffet spends 5 to 6 hours daily reading newspapers. He makes sure to read five different ones. He also goes through 500 pages of investment documents and recommends this to all investors. According to him, knowledge works like that. Like compound interest, it builds up. Everyone can do it, he says, but not many won't do it.

Bill Gates

Formerly the CEO of Microsoft, Bill Gates says that he reads 50 books a year. This roughly translates to one each week.

Most of the books he reads are non-fiction and deal with science, business, engineering, disease, and public health. Occasionally, he reads a novel. However, he is more interested in books that make him more knowledgeable about the world.

Mark Zuckerberg

In 2015, Mike Zuckerberg revealed in a Facebook post that he intends to read a new book each week. He said that he was interested in learning more about technologies, histories, beliefs, and cultures. He said that books cause you to explore something fully and get deeper into it.

Oprah Winfrey

The talk show host has been encouraging her viewers to read since 1996. She says that reading is her path to freedom. For her, books allowed her to see a world beyond her grandmother's house. They opened her eyes to possibilities that went beyond what was acceptable at the time.

Mark Cuban

Mark is the owner of Dallas Mavericks. He is always saying that you should treat your business like a sport. That means looking for the competitive edge in every possible way. For him, it means three hours of reading each day so he can learn about various industries. Mark asserts that this was very fruitful when he was starting his career. All the things he read were public. The books and magazines are accessible to anyone. The information he acquired can be accessed by whoever wants it. However, he says, many are not interested.

David Rubenstein

Rubenstein is the cofounder of The Carlyle Group. He reads about six books every week and almost eight newspapers every day. He attributes this extraordinary ability to his laser-like sense of focus. David says that he has always been driven from an early age.

Phil Knight

This Nike founder had a library at the back of his executive office. He kept it sacred and asked anyone who entered take off their shoes and even bow.

He stepped down as the CEO, but he says that the library still exists.

Elon Musk

Musk co-founded PayPal and is now the CEO of Tesla. However, before all that, he dedicated 10 hours each day to reading science-fiction novels. That is how he became knowledgeable about rockets. You have come across people who look like they have it all together. They happily and successfully manage their responsibilities, careers, and families. How do these people manage to juggle so many things with ease while you can barely do one thing without getting frustrated? These are the same people that win the race, get promoted, never appear stressed, and everyone admires them. This is their secret. They get enough sleep. People who sleep properly are happy, focused, and successful. Sleep helps recharge your body and brain. When you are feeling tired, you will jump from one task to another without clarity. You, like everyone else, want to be the best version of yourself in parenting, your career, or whatever you do. The modern life is so busy, and sleep is a luxury for many people. You always hear the saying "I'll sleep when I'm dead" often. This is a mistake. Sleep is an important factor if you really want to achieve your goals. Poor sleep habits will wear you out. You will begin to break down. You become moody and irritable. If you continue depriving yourself of sleep, you may experience anxiety and hallucinations. You will be emotionally flattened, and your relationships will take a blow. Your ability to remember will lessen, causing cognitive delays. You may get into substance abuse. You may start getting micro-sleep.

Sleep Don'ts

Avoid eating right before bed. Eat three hours before you go to sleep. Stay away from alcohol and caffeine. Alcohol may make you drowsy at first, but it can cause you to wake up many times during the night. Use your bed for sleep only, not TV, not work; just sleep. Turn off the lights. Bright lights repress melatonin, the sleep hormone. Avoid sleeping too much. Oversleeping does more harm than good. Eight hours of sleep is enough for an adult.

What to Do

Meditate: stress is the leading cause of sleeplessness. Learn to turn off your mind.

Positive thinking and organization: before bed, write down all the positive things that happened during your day. Also, make a to-do list for the following day.

Exercise: do this late afternoon or early morning. It makes you feel better and aids sleep.

Hydrate: stay hydrated all through the day.

Relaxation tea: the aroma itself will relax you and get your body ready for bed.

Wake up early: this is a key factor if you want to be successful. It makes you start the day in calmness without rushing.

Maintain a sleep schedule: have a routine. Sleep at the same time and wake up at the same time every day.

Keep your room cool: 65^0F is perfect according to research.

Life goes on: solve what you can and don't worry about what you cannot solve.

Laugh: humor and laughter make you stress less and become more likeable. Have your goals somewhere at your bedside table: When you wake up, it will be the first thing you see every morning.

Conclusion

You will always hear people giving excuses saying that they were not born with the talent necessary to succeed. It is true there are naturally advantaged people in some ways. However, attaining success at something boils down to committing yourself and taking the time to acquire and master skills. In fact, talent is nothing more than a starting point. Nobody is denying that natural talent exists. There are genetically advantaged, especially where physical ability is concerned. Nonetheless, success is not always a physical venture for most people. They just want to do something and be good at it. They desire to earn a decent salary while doing something fulfilling—all for a comfortable life. When that goal is not attained, it is easy to sit on your couch, sulking, and envying those that are successful. You will start wishing that you were blessed with talent as well. You should know that you can make things work in your favor. You must be willing to change. The wrong perspective can have you miss out on so many opportunities. As soon as you make yourself believe that talent is all you need to succeed, you have already put up a wall. You will convince yourself that you cannot get to a certain point because you lack talent. The problem with this kind of thinking is that it assumes that you need innate ability to perform well. This way of thinking will limit you. Sure, talent makes a difference. However, the lack of it will never hinder you from following your talent. You can be a master at a skill without having the natural talent—although you might have to weather a few storms. Dedication and passion are what really matters. Talent can be learnt. Every successful person you see had to work hard to get there; from the Olympic sprinter to the world-renowned musician. Do you desire to be successful? Well, stop limiting yourself. Ability is not talent. Think of abilities as skills. When you refer to talents as skills, you tell your subconscious that it is learnable. If you know and believe that it is possible, you are halfway there. This does not just apply to technical stuff like playing the guitar. Even singing can be learned— and this is supported by science. When everything to you is a skill and not a talent, an entire world of opportunities will open for you. The successful, talented people you see will only be dedicated individuals in your eyes. Rich businessmen/women will be disciplined investors. Famous public speakers will just be people who took time to practice. If you set your mind right, the next half of the battle will be possible to conquer. Know what skills you desire to acquire and start practicing. Have a target and dedicate yourself.

"To be a star, you must shine your own light, follow your own path, and don't worry about darkness, for that is when the stars shine brightest."

-Napoleon Hill

www.ingramcontent.com/pod-product-compliance
Lightning Source LLC
Chambersburg PA
CBHW072242170526
45158CB00002BA/985